D1724340

KETO
WITHOUT COOKING

Perfect LCHF Cookbook to Stay Low Carb or Keto When You Don't Want to Cook

**NO-COOK RECIPES AND 14-DAY MEAL PLAN
FOR BUSY PEOPLE ON KETOGENIC DIET**

Adele Baker

Disclaimer

The recipes and information in this book are provided for educational purposes only. Please always consult a licensed professional before making changes to your lifestyle or diet. The author and publisher shall have neither liability nor responsibility to anyone with respect to any loss or damage caused or alleged to be caused directly or indirectly by the information contained in this book. All trademarks and brands within this book are for clarifying purposes only and are owned by the owners themselves, not affiliated with this document.

Images from shutterstock.com

CONTENTS

INTRODUCTION

Sometimes, you don't really want to cook — maybe because you're too exhausted or just don't feel like cooking — but you still need to feed yourself and your family. What you need is a simple, fulfilling meal without a lot of effort.

It may be after a long and hard day at work or just a bad day – it doesn't matter – this book is designed to always help you.

With its recipes, it will be a helping hand in the aforementioned situations, giving you "eureka" what-to-cook ideas and ways to implement them when you need it the most.

In addition to that, it provides a meal plan and various tips that are there to save time and bring certainty to your life.

And to find this, simply flip this page and get started.

CHAPTER 1. HOW CAN I DIET WITHOUT COOKING?

NO-COOK KETO MEALS - HOW TO EAT LOW CARB WITHOUT COOKING

Many people get frustrated, confused, or overwhelmed at the prospect of having to learn all the new recipes to cook when they begin their ketogenic diet. They end up browsing all the recipe sites around, and sometimes they don't even get started on the actual diet until they think they're "ready" with enough recipes.

They say they will never do keto since they don't have time to make their own "false bread," or they don't know how to cook, so they just keep on eating all the carb-filled junk foods.

People often assume that keto means making your own mayonnaise, or having to look for special butter from only the most sacred of grass-fed cows every single time to do all kinds

of fancy stuff with your coffee, or to spend endless hours trying to make your own cauliflower rice in a food processor...

But in reality, that's not the point of keto. Keto can be very easy (and should be.) But for some reason, many people love making things much more difficult than they need to be.

You desperately want to eat healthier, have no time to cook, and your lack of energy leads to junk food?

It is entirely possible to follow a strict ketogenic diet even without cooking at all! In a few pages, this book will demonstrate this with its recipes.

TIME SAVING TIPS

If we are frank, most of us run around like headless free-range chickens. From this, we drive to that, working too late and overbooking our calendars. We are drowning in emails, exhausted by commitments, glued to screens, gasping for air because there are not enough hours in the day.

These time-saving tips will reduce unnecessary time wasting and help you get the most out of every second you've been spending in your kitchen:

GET ORGANIZED

Organizing in the kitchen is a very tangible way to save time every day. It's going to save more time than anything else.

Here are ideas for layout that really make a huge difference:

- Stack your plates/tassels/cutlery as close as possible to the dishwasher/sink.
- Putting plates away after they have been cleaned saves a massive amount of time.
- Put the most frequently used items in easy reach, and the least frequently used items farther away.
- When it comes to food storage – use the right containers for the job – that means you waste less time opening and closing unfitting lids, or tapping disposable grocery bags, etc.

PLAN WELL

There's no bigger time waster than going to the kitchen to prepare the tea and realizing you've run out of a crucial thing...

The time it takes to get to the store, or even to figure out what you can cook is massive, and it really piles up over the days/weeks. The answer? Figure it out as best as you can beforehand.

It can mean a few things:

- Meal Plan – know what you're going to cook up front, so there's plenty of time for you to sort it out.
- Shopping List – Use your meal plan to know exactly what you will need for each meal, so you are less likely to miss something
- Take stuff out of the freezer beforehand, so you don't have to wait for it to thaw or worry about something else to cook...
- Think about the leftovers – if you intend to

use the leftovers for lunch the next day from the evening meal, you will save tons of time by not having to cook a lot for that meal.

PREP WELL

Preparation is essential for saving time, in addition to planning well.

- Prepare all the meals for a week in one sitting – that way, you have it all out, and if you prepare everything on your least busy day, you'll save a lot of extra time in a week.
- If you don't want to prepare all your meals, why don't you cut all the fruit and vegetables and salad and put them in the refrigerator, ready for any food you've got later in the week?
- If you have a couple of meals with identical ingredients, then why not cook them simultaneously?

WASH & CLEAR AS YOU GO

Nothing is worse than finishing a nice meal and taking the plates to the kitchen just to find out what can be summarized as a bomb site!

Not only is clearing up after you've eaten is the last thing you're going to want to do, the food has probably congealed and stuck hard to the saucepans and the work surface, so you've got to spend even longer clearing it all away.

The trick is to clear as you go. Have a garbage bag near to hand to put peelings, wrappers etc. straight into it. Fill the dishwasher as you go, clean cans for recycling as you are using them.

It all adds up – but doing it as you go means that at the end of the meal, you will only be left with the plates and the cutlery.

USE FOOD SHORTCUTS

Using some food shortcuts is not a bad thing...

- Do not use new recipes. You need to worry about-recipes that have been tried and tested and will save you time.
- Frozen veg is good, generally better for you as they are frozen when picked and have had little time to lose the nutrients – plus, they're fast and easy to handle.
- If you have the time, get salad bags and pre-prepared food.

CHAPTER 2. NO COOK KETO MEAL PLAN

DAY 1

Breakfast

Berry Arugula Breakfast Bowl (p. 16)
Green Low Carb Smoothie (p. 34)

Calories - 755	Carbohydrates – 9 g
	Fat – 57 g
	Protein – 44 g

Lunch

Keto Buddha Bowl (p. 23)

Calories - 232	Carbohydrates – 7 g
	Fat – 19 g
	Protein – 4 g

Dinner

Keto Cobb Bowl (p. 28)

Calories - 557	Carbohydrates – 7 g
	Fat – 48 g
	Protein – 21 g

DAY 2

Breakfast

Yogurt Parfait (p. 17)
Keto Iced Tea Cocktail (p. 35)

Calories - 534	Carbohydrates – 25 g
	Fat – 27 g
	Protein – 49 g

Lunch

Green Veggies and Tofu Bowl (p. 24)

Calories – 289	Carbohydrates – 5 g
	Fat – 20 g
	Protein – 15 g

Dinner

Tuna Crunchy Bowl (p. 29)

Calories - 500	Carbohydrates – 18 g
	Fat – 40 g
	Protein – 53 g

DAY 3

Breakfast

Matcha Orange Breakfast Bowl (p. 18)
Raspberry Avocado Smoothie (p. 36)

Calories - 481	Carbohydrates – 18 g
	Fat – 30 g
	Protein – 7 g

Lunch

Rainbow Salad Bowl (p. 25)

Calories - 138	Carbohydrates – 7 g
	Fat – 12 g
	Protein – 3 g

Dinner

Sushi Bowl (p. 30)

Calories - 339	Carbohydrates – 4 g
	Fat – 19 g
	Protein – 36 g

DAY 4

Breakfast

Kiwi Smoothie Bowl (p. 19)

Calories - 570	Carbohydrates – 4 g
	Fat – 35 g
	Protein – 35 g

Lunch

Ahi Poke Tuna Bowl (p. 26)

Calories - 377	Carbohydrates – 9 g
	Fat – 20 g
	Protein – 35 g

Dinner

Turkey Roll-Ups (p. 31)

Calories - 345	Carbohydrates – 6 g
	Fat – 23 g
	Protein – 35 g

DAY 5

Breakfast

Strawberry Chia Pudding (p. 29)
Strawberry Basil Italian Lemonade (p. 58)

Calories - 230	Carbohydrates – 6 g
	Fat – 18 g
	Protein – 5 g

Lunch

Caprese Bowl with Pesto and Bacon (p. 39)

Calories - 153	Carbohydrates – 3 g
	Fat – 12 g
	Protein – 7 g

Dinner

Mediterranean Collard Green Wraps (p. 49)

Calories - 208	Carbohydrates – 9 g
	Fat – 17 g
	Protein – 4 g

DAY 6

Breakfast

Egg and Spinach Mug (p. 21)
Chocolate Mint Avocado Smoothie (p. 39)

Calories - 691	Carbohydrates – 15 g
	Fat – 70 g
	Protein – 43 g

Lunch

Green Veggies and Tofu Bowl (p. 24)

Calories - 289	Carbohydrates – 5 g
	Fat – 20 g
	Protein – 15 g

Dinner

Keto Tabbouleh (p. 33)

Calories - 369	Carbohydrates – 6 g
	Fat – 32 g
	Protein – 13 g

DAY 7

Breakfast

Raspberry Pudding Bowl (p. 22)
Strawberry Limeade (p. 40)

Calories - 365	Carbohydrates – 28 g
	Fat – 36 g
	Protein – 44 g

Lunch

Keto Buddha Bowl (p. 23)

Calories - 232	Carbohydrates – 7 g
	Fat – 19 g
	Protein – 4 g

Dinner

Keto Cobb Bowl (p. 28)

Calories - 557	Carbohydrates – 7 g
	Fat – 48 g
	Protein – 21 g

DAY 8

Breakfast

Avocado Turkey Toasts (p. 53)
Keto Iced Tea Cocktail (p. 35)

Calories - 956	Carbohydrates – 24 g
	Fat – 70 g
	Protein – 57 g

Lunch

Smoked Salmon and Avocado Caesar Salad (p. 43)

Calories - 497	Carbohydrates – 16 g
	Fat – 25 g
	Protein – 26 g

Dinner

Sushi Bowl (p. 30)

Calories - 339	Carbohydrates – 4 g
	Fat – 19 g
	Protein – 36 g

DAY 9

Breakfast

Matcha Orange Breakfast Bowl (p. 18)
Raspberry Avocado Smoothie (p. 36)

Calories - 481	Carbohydrates – 18 g
	Fat – 30 g
	Protein – 7 g

Lunch

Lunch Salad with Tuna (p. 44)

Calories - 464	Carbohydrates – 4 g
	Fat – 32 g
	Protein – 39 g

Dinner

Turkey Roll-Ups (p. 31)

Calories - 345	Carbohydrates – 6 g
	Fat – 23 g
	Protein – 35 g

DAY 10

Breakfast

Yogurt Parfait (p. 17)
Green Low Carb Smoothie (p. 34)

Calories - 613	Carbohydrates – 12 g
	Fat – 42 g
	Protein – 42 g

Lunch

Salmon, Avocado and Arugula Salad (p. 45)

Calories - 575	Carbohydrates – 11 g
	Fat – 49 g
	Protein – 25 g

Dinner

Mediterranean Collard Green Wraps (p. 32)

Calories - 208	Carbohydrates – 9 g
	Fat – 17 g
	Protein – 4 g

DAY 11

Breakfast

Strawberry Chia Pudding (p. 20)
Strawberry Limeade (p. 40)

Calories - 384	Carbohydrates – 14 g
	Fat – 34 g
	Protein – 40 g

Lunch

Keto Tuna Salad with Avocado (p. 46)

Calories - 297	Carbohydrates – 7 g
	Fat – 13 g
	Protein – 34 g

Dinner

Keto Tabbouleh (p. 33)

Calories - 369	Carbohydrates – 6 g
	Fat – 32 g
	Protein – 13 g

DAY 12

Breakfast

Egg and Spinach Mug (p. 21)
Chocolate Mint Avocado Smoothie (p. 39)

Calories - 691	Carbohydrates – 15 g
	Fat – 70 g
	Protein – 43 g

Lunch

Strawberry Spinach Salad (p. 47)

Calories - 267	Carbohydrates – 8 g
	Fat – 26 g
	Protein – 3 g

Dinner

Keto Cobb Bowl (p. 28)

Calories - 557	Carbohydrates – 7 g
	Fat – 48 g
	Protein – 21 g

DAY 13

Breakfast

Kiwi Smoothie Bowl (p. 19)

Calories - 570	Carbohydrates – 4 g
	Fat – 35 g
	Protein – 35 g

Lunch

Green Veggies and Tofu Bowl (p. 24)

Calories - 289	Carbohydrates – 5 g
	Fat – 20 g
	Protein – 15 g

Dinner

Tuna Crunchy Bowl (p. 29)

Calories - 500	Carbohydrates – 18 g
	Fat – 40 g
	Protein – 53 g

DAY 14

Breakfast

Raspberry Pudding Bowl (p. 22)
Strawberry Basil Italian Lemonade (p. 38)

Calories - 356	Carbohydrates – 20 g
	Fat – 20 g
	Protein – 9 g

Lunch

Keto Buddha Bowl (p. 23)

Calories - 232	Carbohydrates – 7 g
	Fat – 19 g
	Protein – 4 g

Dinner

Ahi Poke Tuna Bowl (p. 26)

Calories - 377	Carbohydrates – 9 g
	Fat – 20 g
	Protein – 35 g

CHAPTER 3. SHOPPING GUIDE

GROCERY GUIDE

It all starts at the grocery shop. If you want a keto diet to be effective, you need to know how to shop for keto groceries.

These are the three most common mistakes that all people make while buying food for a keto diet, and how they can be avoided.

1. HIGHLY PROCESSED FOOD

Even on a keto diet, you can buy unsafe food. But not if you keep it "real." Here's how:

BUY WHOLE FOOD
Whole food comes with just one ingredient. Examples include meat, seafood, eggs, butter, oils, fruit, vegetables, and nuts. They should form the basis of your keto diet. And so many delicious choices!!

LIMIT PACKAGED FOOD

Most of the packaged food products you'll find in grocery stores are highly processed. Often, they're full of sugar and starch too. For this reason, a keto diet should reduce them to a minimum.

Fortunately, you can easily avoid highly processed food. Here's how:

IGNORE THE OBVIOUS
There are moments when the package speaks for itself. If it says something like "cereal," "cake," "cookie," "bread," or "chips"—do not read anymore. Just walk away. Since these foods are high in carbs, they're not the right choice on a keto diet.

IGNORE LOW-CARB PRODUCTS
If your supermarket sells low-carb varieties of pastas, breads, and cookies, avoiding them is

usually advised. Many contain starch and other additives. Some contain sweeteners, which could hinder your development.

IGNORE "NATURAL" OR "HEALTHY" LABELS

Many food products that are highly processed are labeled "healthy" or "natural." Ignore these meaningless terms. Note any health claims, including Heart-Check AHA. Stick as much as possible with single-ingredient, savory keto foods.

BUY MINIMALLY-PROCESSED PACKAGED FOODS

Not all packaged foods are highly processed, but how do you know which to trust?

Eggs, meat, and fish are great choices, although often packed.

Some foods that are minimally processed are packaged while still being keto-friendly. Butter, cheese, coconut oil, olive oil, milk, nut butter, shredded veggies (like coleslaw), and sour milk are included.

Some slightly more processed foods may also be all right. Choose beef jerky, hollandaise, pesto, pizza sauce, salad dressings, bacon, tahini, and tapenade, with no-sugar-added. Check the list of ingredients and the carbohydrate content, as carbs and additives differ from one brand to another.

2. TOO MANY CARBOHYDRATES

Now, understanding how to eliminate highly processed food, let's address the second keto grocery error: too many carbs.

It is preferable to eat a maximum of 20 grams of net carbs per day for keto results. Here's how carbs won't creep into your house:

AVOID CARB CREEP

Carbs add up. You ate the broccoli and carrots for dinner, those whipped-cream strawberries you had for dessert, and nuts and dark chocolate that you enjoyed earlier in the day-they all add up.

Even eating healthy keto foods could take you out of ketosis, "a little bit of this" and "a little bit of that." If you don't get results on your keto diet, take these tips for grocery shopping:

FEWER HIGH-CARB VEGETABLES

Do not stock up on high-carb vegetables. Leafy greens, asparagus, avocado, and courgettes come to mind. You can enjoy other tasty veggies instead such as broccoli, cauliflower, green beans, and brussels. But be a little bit careful with them, because they still contain a few carbs.

BUY LESS FRUIT

Your best bet on a keto diet is to avoid buying any fruit. If you want to eat some occasionally, although no fruit is good for keto, strawberries, raspberries, and blackberries are all right, especially if you keep the serving size low. Lemon and lime work in small quantities too.

BUY LESS DARK CHOCOLATE AND FEWER NUTS

Nuts and dark chocolate in limited portions are keto-friendly, but since they're both handy and tasty, overeating these treats can be easy and you will end up going over your daily carb limit. So, it's better to, for example, opt for macadamia nuts or pecans rather than cashews because they contain fewer carbs.

3. POTENTIALLY UNHEALTHY INGREDIENTS

Nearly all packaged goods come with a list of ingredients. Before buying something new, always make sure to try it out.

AVOID SUGAR

Try to eliminate sugar in all its types when making keto-selections. Sometimes manufacturers come up with unusual names to mask the sugar on their labels. Generally, avoid:

- A sugar, syrup, malt or cane product of some sort
- Any chemical that ends with 'ose' (as with lactose)
- All natural sugars such as honey, fruit juice concentrate, and dried fruit.

AVOID GRAINS

In our diets, most of the starch comes from grains. The main ones are wheat and corn, but any type of grain or flour (except nut flour) add carbohydrates to a food product. For keto eaters, this can spell trouble.

AVOID ARTIFICIAL SWEETENERS AND OTHER CHEMICALS

Low-carb sweeteners can potentially decrease weight loss and trigger sweet cravings. We recommend to remove them from your keto diet and help ban sugar cravings for good.

AVOID TRANS FATS AND HIGHLY-PROCESSED VEGETABLE OILS

While keto accentuates fat, not all fats are created equal. Place naturally occurring fats in your cart and stay away from altered and industrial fats.

Avoid anything partially hydrogenated or any ingredients like margarine or shortening. Research shows these fats may have adverse effects on heart health.

Limit highly processed vegetable seed oils — canola, maize, cottonseed, grapeseed, safflower, and soybean oils because they are highly processed and rich in fatty acids omega-6.

While both omega-6 and omega-3 fats are important, meaning we need to get them from food, today, most diets have far more omega-6 than we need. Moreover, the impact of vegetable oils on wellbeing is still uncertain.

ESSENTIAL SHOPPING LIST

A reliable keto diet food list allows you to plan your meals for the week. Each time you shop in a grocery store, a final food list ensures that you make the right choices and stay in ketosis.

Regardless of whether you plan to start your diet soon or are already in ketosis, this shopping list is your helper. I divided it into different categories, making it easy for you to choose the items that you'd like to eat during the week.

Fats

What is a keto diet without fat? Typically, 75% of your meal in a day should include just fats. Here are some great fat options to choose from.

AVOCADOES

Avocadoes are super healthy, and it is quite easy to get hold of them in India now. All stores stock these up, thanks to the demand. You can buy 1-2 medium-sized avocadoes for the week. Make sure one is riper than the other to ensure you have enough fruit throughout the week.

CHEESE

You just cannot have enough of cheese when on keto. Many people bake cheese on a large tray and use it like how they would use flatbread. Cheese wraps with fillings are great options for lunch.

COTTAGE CHEESE

Also popularly known as paneer, you can make a variety of Indian and continental dishes with paneer cubes. These can also be frozen and used any time you want. 1kg of paneer should be enough to take you through the week.

BUTTER

Butter is a perfect ingredient to sauté all your food in or to add in soups and stews. It is a good way to add fat content to whatever you eat. If you drink bullet coffee every morning, a dollop of butter to it makes it very filling and satisfying.

CREAM

Add a tetra pack each of both coconut cream and fresh cream to your shopping bag. If you are a fan of sweet treats, then these creams can be used to whip up tasty desserts.

Proteins

Protein is very important to prevent you from losing muscle mass and to keep your hair and nails healthy. Proteins also give you the strength to go through the day without feeling tired. Some of the common protein sources you should buy are mentioned here.

MEAT

If you enjoy meat, pork, chicken, and lamb have to be on your shopping list. It will be more affordable and tastier if you rotate the meats over the week. If you choose lamb and pork for this week, pick chicken and pork for the next.

SEAFOOD

Seafood is also protein-rich, and it can be converted into amazing meals every day. All types of fish are great when on a keto diet. Fish can be fried, steamed, or made into curries that you can enjoy with cauliflower rice.

EGGS

No keto lover's shopping list is complete without eggs. Eggs can be had for breakfast, lunch, dinner, or even as snacks. If you are hungry and are in no mood to cook, a couple of boiled eggs dipped in salt and pepper makes a satisfying meal. The protein from the egg will keep you very healthy too.

YOGURT

Yogurt is a great source of protein too. A cup of yogurt mixed with a handful of berries can make an instant breakfast. Add a couple of packs of yogurt to your shopping list.

SPICES AND CONDIMENTS

Always have a stock of chili powder, salt, turmeric, garam masala, cinnamon powder, onion and garlic powder, oregano seasonings, pepper powder, and cajun spice. You can make almost any dish appetizing with these spices.

SAUCES AND DIPS

Sauces and dips are very important to enhance the taste of the dish you cook. Sauces can make simple soups and salads taste amazing. Many generic sauce mixes are full of sugar, though. Check the ingredients added and the nutritional values before picking the below sauces.

- Red chili sauce
- Soy sauce
- Mayonnaise
- Balsamic vinegar
- Lemon-avocado sauce
- Ranch sauce

Cooking oil

Some of the top keto cooking oils you need to have in your shopping cart are:

- Coconut oil
- Avocado oil
- Olive oil

You can use coconut oil for all types of deep-frying, sautéing, and shallow frying, and bacon fat oil tastes amazing when you fry aromatic spices and condiments. Olive oil is lighter and can be used to make salads, omelets, and soups.

Vegetables and fruits

Here is a list of all allowed vegetables and fruit for a keto diet. You can choose the ones you prefer and buy them for the week. It is important to rotate your veggie and fruit choices every week. This way, you will get the micronutrients offered by all the vegetables and fruit instead of restricting your diet with the same choices.

- Cauliflower
- Cabbage
- Tomatoes
- Peppers
- Mushrooms
- Spinach (Palak)
- Other types of greens
- Lettuce
- All kinds of berries
- Apples
- Avocados
- Lemons

Snacks

Many people get hungry between meals, especially in the evenings, and are unsure what to munch on. Here is what you can buy and stock up over the weekend to help you handle hunger between meals.

- Avocado toast
- Roasted dry nuts like walnuts, almonds, pecan nuts
- Macadamia nuts
- Fat bombs
- Plates with veggies and protein
- Dried berries (unsweetened)
- Lemonade.

BERRY ARUGULA BREAKFAST BOWL

SERVINGS: 1 PREP TIME: 5 min. COOK TIME: 5 min.

CARBS – 5 g   FAT – 32 g   PROTEIN – 16 g   CALORIES – 380

Ingredients

- 2 cups arugula, kale, spinach, power greens
- ¼ cup raspberries or strawberries
- 2 Tbsp nuts or seeds
- 2 slices bacon
- 1-2 Tbsp balsamic dressing (p. 63)

Directions

1. Start by choosing any type of greens.
2. Add raspberries or strawberries to the greens.
3. Add nuts or seeds, then add the bacon.
4. Drizzle with balsamic dressing and toss well.

YOGURT PARFAIT

SERVINGS: 1   PREP TIME: 5 min.   COOK TIME: 00 min.

CARBS – 8 g   FAT – 17 g   PROTEIN – 14 g   CALORIES – 238

Ingredients

- *2 Tbsp raw mixed nuts, chopped*
- *¼ cup fresh berries*
- *1 cup good non-dairy yogurt*

Directions

1. Layer the nuts, berries and yogurt in a glass bowl.
2. Top with a few berries and nuts before serving.

MATCHA ORANGE BREAKFAST BOWL

SERVINGS: 1   PREP TIME: 10 min.   COOK TIME: 00 min.

CARBS – 9 g   FAT – 10 g   PROTEIN – 5 g   CALORIES – 151

Ingredients

- *1 cup plant milk*
- *2 Tbsp chia seeds*
- *¼-½ avocado*
- *⅛ cup fresh mint leaves*
- *1-2 tsp matcha*
- *Vanilla stevia drops, to taste*
- *1 pinch pink Himalayan salt*
- *1 blood orange, peeled and sliced*
- *Nuts of choice, chopped*

Directions

1. Mix the chia seeds with milk, sweetener, matcha, and salt. Cover and refrigerate overnight.
2. Add some avocado, mint, and a handful of ice and transfer to a blender.
3. Blend on high speed until smooth.
4. Serve with orange slices and chopped nuts on top.

KIWI SMOOTHIE BOWL

SERVINGS: 1 PREP TIME: 5 min. COOK TIME: 00 min.

CARBS – 4 g FAT – 35 g PROTEIN – 35 g CALORIES – 570

Ingredients

- 1 cup spinach
- ½ cup almond milk
- 2 Tbsp non-dairy heavy cream
- 1 Tbsp coconut oil
- 1 scoop low carb protein powder
- 2 ice cubes
- 1 kiwi, sliced
- ¼ cup blueberries
- 1 Tbsp shredded coconut
- 1 tsp chia seeds

Directions

1. Add the spinach to the blender, then add milk, cream, coconut oil, and ice.
2. Blend until everything is combined and has an even consistency.
3. Transfer to a bowl and top with kiwi, blueberry, seeds, and shredded coconut.

STRAWBERRY CHIA PUDDING

SERVINGS: 1 PREP TIME: 35 min. COOK TIME: 00 min.

CARBS – 4 g FAT – 18 g PROTEIN – 5 g CALORIES – 223

Ingredients

- *1 cup coconut milk*
- *½ cup almond milk*
- *1 cup fresh or frozen strawberries*
- *½ cup whole chia seeds*
- *1 tsp vanilla powder*
- *Stevia, to taste*

Directions

1. Put the milk, water, and berries into a blender and pulse until blended.
2. Mix the chia seeds, strawberry milk, vanilla, and stevia.
3. Let it sit for 25-30 minutes or refrigerate overnight.
4. Serve with a strawberry half on top.

EGG AND SPINACH MUG

SERVINGS: 1 PREP TIME: 10 min. COOK TIME: 00 min.

CARBS – 5 g FAT – 26 g PROTEIN – 17 g CALORIES – 139

Ingredients

- *2 large eggs*
- *⅛ tsp kosher salt*
- *⅛ tsp black pepper*
- *2 Tbsp shredded cheddar cheese*
- *½ cup spinach*

Directions

1. Beat the eggs in a microwave safe bowl. Add the milk, and continue beating with fork.
2. Add the cheese, spinach, salt, and pepper.
3. Put in the microwave. Cook on high for 1-2 minutes. Stir and enjoy. Cook for 30-45 seconds more, if it's not cooked through.

RASPBERRY PUDDING BOWL

SERVINGS: 3 PREP TIME: 5 min. COOK TIME: 00 min.

CARBS – 18 g FAT – 20 g PROTEIN – 9 g CALORIES – 349

Ingredients

- 1½ cup full-fat coconut milk
- 1 cup frozen raspberries
- ¼ cup MCT oil
- 2 Tbsp chia seeds
- 1 Tbsp apple cider vinegar
- 1 tsp vanilla extract
- 3 drops stevia
- 1 Tbsp shredded coconut
- ¼ cup fresh berries for serving
- 1 sliced banana for serving

Directions

1. Add all of the pudding ingredients (except the banana, fresh berries, and coconut) in a blender. Blend until smooth, for 1 minute.
2. Serve and top with fresh berries and fruit. Sprinkle with coconut flakes.

KETO BUDDHA BOWL

SERVINGS: 1 PREP TIME: 10 min. COOK TIME: 00 min.

CARBS – 7 g FAT – 19 g PROTEIN – 4 g CALORIES – 232

Ingredients

- 1 cup arugula
- 1 cup mushrooms of your choice (optional)
- 1 tsp lime juice raw
- ½ cup raw or cooked cauliflower rice
- ¼ cup, sliced cucumber
- ½ halved avocado
- ⅛ tsp salt
- ⅛ tsp black pepper
- 2 tsp olive oil
- 1 pinch sesame seeds

Directions

1. Assemble your bowls by combining all of the ingredients together and serve.

GREEN VEGGIES AND TOFU BOWL

SERVINGS: 1 PREP TIME: 10 min. COOK TIME: 00 min.

CARBS – 5 g FAT – 20 g PROTEIN – 15 g CALORIES – 289

Ingredients

- ½ cup cooked or raw cauliflower rice
- 1 cup watercress
- ¼ cup edamame beans
- 1 cup tofu
- ¼ cup cucumber cubes
- ¼ avocado, sliced
- 1 tsp sesame seeds

Directions

1. Combine all of the components in a bowl, sprinkle with sesame seeds and enjoy.

RAINBOW SALAD BOWL

SERVINGS: 6 PREP TIME: 10 min. COOK TIME: 00 min.

CARBS – 7 g FAT – 12 g PROTEIN – 3 g CALORIES – 138

Ingredients

- *4 cups spinach*
- *½ medium avocado, cubed*
- *½ cup red cabbage, shredded*
- *½ cup pomegranate arils*
- *¼ cup peaches, quartered*
- *¼ cubed feta cheese (optional)*
- *1-2 Tbsp pomegranate balsamic vinaigrette dressing (p. 63)*

Directions

1. Toss the dressing with the spinach until evenly coated.
2. Add the rest of the ingredients and toss the salad to combine.

AHI POKE TUNA BOWL

SERVINGS: 1 PREP TIME: 2 h. 10 min. COOK TIME: 00 min.

CARBS – 9 g FAT – 20 g PROTEIN – 35 g CALORIES – 377

Ingredients

FOR THE MARINADE:
- 4 oz raw tuna, cut into bite-size cubes
- 2 Tbsp liquid aminos
- 1 tsp sesame oil
- 1 tsp rice wine vinegar
- 1 tsp chili garlic sauce
- 1 drop liquid stevia

FOR THE BOWL:
- ¼ cup cucumber, sliced
- ½ medium avocado, sliced
- 1 cups leafy greens
- ½ tsp sesame oil
- ½ tsp rice wine vinegar
- ¼ tsp sesame seeds
- 1 Tbsp scallions, chopped

Directions

1. Add all of the marinade to a bowl and toss in the tuna. Cover with plastic wrap over the bowl and leave in the fridge for 2 hours.
2. Add the greens to another bowl and drizzle with the sesame oil and vinegar. Toss well.
3. Put the cucumber and avocado slices on top.
4. Remove the excess marinade and add the tuna into the bowl with the vegetables.
5. Top with sesame seeds and scallions.

CAPRESE BOWL WITH PESTO AND BACON

SERVINGS: 2 PREP TIME: 15 min. COOK TIME: 00 min.

CARBS – 3 g FAT – 12 g PROTEIN – 7 g CALORIES – 153

Ingredients

- *10 oz grape tomatoes*
- *5 slices bacon, cut into pieces*
- *½ oz fresh basil*
- *10 oz fresh mozzarella balls*
- *¼ cup basil pesto*
- *2 Tbsp olive oil*
- *Black pepper, to taste*

Directions

1. Skewer the tomatoes, bacon pieces, fresh basil, and mozzarella balls onto the toothpicks, in that order. (You can fold any larger basil pieces as needed.)
2. In a small bowl, whisk the pesto and olive oil. If it's still thick, thin out with more oil.
3. Drizzle the pesto over the skewers. Top with fresh ground pepper.

KETO COBB BOWL

SERVINGS: 4 PREP TIME: 20 min. COOK TIME: 00 min.

CARBS – 7 g FAT – 48 g PROTEIN – 21 g CALORIES – 557

Ingredients

- ¾-oz slices bacon, chopped
- 5 oz deli turkey
- 3 Tbsp olive oil mayonnaise, divided
- Sea salt and black pepper, to taste
- 2 hard-boiled eggs (optional)
- 1 cup finely chopped romaine lettuce
- 1 avocado, sliced
- ½ cup halved cherry tomatoes
- ¼ cup diced green onions
- 1 cup dairy-free ranch dressing

Directions

1. Add the turkey to a bowl and stir in 2 Tbsp mayonnaise, salt, and pepper.
2. In another bowl, mash the eggs with 1 Tbsp mayonnaise, and season with salt and pepper. (Optional step)
3. Add the lettuce to the bottom of the serving bowls. Divide the avocado, turkey, and egg mixture between bowls evenly. Top each bowl with tomato, bacon, and green onions.
4. Drizzle each bowl with 2 Tbsp dressing.

TUNA CRUNCHY BOWL

SERVINGS: 2 PREP TIME: 10 min. COOK TIME: 00 min.

CARBS – 18 g FAT – 40 g PROTEIN – 53 g CALORIES – 500

Ingredients

- 8 oz fresh salmon or tuna, cubed
- 1 Tbsp sesame oil
- 1 tsp soy sauce, or tamari
- Salt, to taste
- 6 oz cabbage, thinly sliced
- 4 oz cucumber, sliced
- ½ medium avocado, diced
- ¼ cup cilantro
- 2 Tbsp mayonnaise
- 1 tsp soy sauce
- 2 drops liquid stevia
- 1 Tbsp black sesame seeds

Directions

1. Put the salmon cubes into a bowl.
2. Add the sesame oil, soy sauce, and salt. Mix well. Set aside to let salmon marinate for 10-15 minutes.
3. Put the cucumber, cabbage, avocado, and cilantro in the bottom of a serving bowl.
4. Mix the mayonnaise, soy sauce, and stevia in a small bowl.
5. Arrange the salmon over the vegetables.
6. Drizzle with the dressing, then sprinkle sesame seeds on top.

SUSHI BOWL

SERVINGS: 2 PREP TIME: 15 min. COOK TIME: 00 min.

CARBS – 4 g FAT – 19 g PROTEIN – 36 g CALORIES – 339

Ingredients

- ¾ lb. mix of salmon and tuna, cut into ½ inch cubes
- ¼ Tbsp chili sauce
- 1 ½ Tbsp soy sauce
- 1 Tbsp sesame oil
- ¼ cup green onions, chopped
- ½ Tbsp sesame seeds
- ¼ cup edamame beans
- ¼ cup seaweed salad
- ¼ cup radish, sliced
- ¼ cup masago
- ¼ avocado, sliced thinly
- 1 cucumber, thinly sliced
- 1 tsp salt
- ½ Tbsp rice vinegar

Directions

1. Toss the tuna and salmon with the sesame oil, soy sauce, green onions, and chili sauce in a bowl. Let it marinate for 15-30 minutes.
2. Dice the cucumber with a sharp knife. Add the rice vinegar and salt to a medium bowl, toss well.
3. Add the fish, cucumber, and the rest of the ingredients to a serving bowl. Drizzle over the extra sauce.

TURKEY ROLL-UPS

SERVINGS: 4 PREP TIME: 10 min. COOK TIME: 00 min.

CARBS – 6 g FAT – 23 g PROTEIN – 35 g CALORIES – 345

Ingredients

FOR THE SPREAD:
- *1 cup non-dairy cream cheese*
- *¼ cup minced shallots*
- *2 Tbsp minced chives*
- *1 pinch of sea salt*

FOR THE ROLLS:
- *1 lb. deli turkey*
- *1 red bell pepper, thinly sliced*
- *1 cucumber, thinly sliced*
- *½ cup greens of choice*

Directions

1. Combine the components for the spread in a small bowl.
2. Place a turkey slice down and top with 1 Tbsp of spread, cucumber, peppers, and greens.
3. Roll it up and slice in half. Repeat with the rest of the turkey and serve.

MEDITERRANEAN COLLARD GREEN WRAPS

SERVINGS: 4   PREP TIME: 15 min.   COOK TIME: 00 min.

CARBS – 9 g   FAT – 17 g   PROTEIN – 4 g   CALORIES – 208

Ingredients

- 4 collard leaves, washed and dried
- ½ cup cauliflower hummus
- 1 cucumber cut into thin, short strips
- ¼ cup red onion, sliced
- 1 bell pepper cut into thin, short strips
- 1 Roma tomato, diced
- 1 avocado, sliced

Directions

1. Shave off the thick part of the collard green stems.
2. Lay out the leaves and spread 2 Tbsp of hummus on each.
3. Top with the cucumbers, peppers, onions, tomatoes, and avocado.
4. Wrap them, beginning from the wide side. Roll them up like a burrito.
5. Place the seam side down and do the same with the rest of wraps.

KETO TABBOULEH

SERVINGS: 6   PREP TIME: 15 min.   COOK TIME: 00 min.

CARBS – 6 g   FAT – 32 g   PROTEIN – 13 g   CALORIES – 369

Ingredients

- ½ cup extra-virgin olive oil
- ¼ cup lemon juice
- ½ tsp sea salt
- 2 bunches fresh parsley, chopped
- 1⅓ cup Manitoba Harvest Hemp Hearts
- 3 tomatoes, diced
- 8 green onions, finely diced
- ¼ cup chopped fresh mint
- 1 small garlic clove, minced

Directions

1. Add the olive oil, lemon juice, and salt to a large bowl. Mix well to combine.
2. Add the rest of the ingredients of tabbouleh, toss to coat well, and serve.

GREEN LOW CARB SMOOTHIE

SERVINGS: 1   PREP TIME: 5 min.   COOK TIME: 00 min.

CARBS – 4 g   FAT – 25 g   PROTEIN – 28 g   CALORIES – 375

Ingredients

- *1½ cups almond milk*
- *1 oz spinach*
- *¼ cup cucumber*
- *¼ cup celery*
- *¼ cup avocado*
- *1 Tbsp coconut oil*
- *10 drops liquid stevia*
- *1 scoop protein powder*
- *½ tsp chia seeds*

Directions

1. Add the milk and spinach to a blender. Blend for a few seconds to break down the spinach leaves.
2. Add in the rest of the ingredients (except the seeds) and blend for 1 minute until smooth.
3. Garnish with chia seeds and serve.

KETO ICED TEA COCKTAIL

SERVINGS: 1   PREP TIME: 5 min.   COOK TIME: 00 min.

CARBS – 17 g FAT – 10 g PROTEIN – 35 g CALORIES – 296

Ingredients

- *½ ounce vodka*
- *½ ounce silver tequila*
- *½ ounce gin*
- *½ ounce light rum*
- *1½ ounces sweet and sour*
- *⅛ tsp orange extract*
- *2½ ounces diet coke*
- *1 cup ice cubes*

Directions

1. Pour all of the liquids (except the diet coke) into a shaker, add ice and shake.
2. Pour into a glass and pour the diet coke over it. Mix and serve cold with a lemon.

RASPBERRY AVOCADO SMOOTHIE

SERVINGS: 2 PREP TIME: 5 min. COOK TIME: 00 min.

CARBS – 9 g FAT – 20 g PROTEIN – 2 g CALORIES – 330

Ingredients

- 1 ripe avocado, peeled and pit removed
- 1⅓ cup water
- 2-3 Tbsp lemon juice
- 2 Tbsp stevia
- ½ cup frozen raspberries
- 1 tsp coconut flakes, for topping

Directions

1. Add all of the ingredients to blender.
2. Blend until smooth for 30 seconds – 1 minute or more.
3. Top with more raspberries and sprinkle with coconut flakes.

KETO MARGARITA

SERVINGS: 1 PREP TIME: 5 min. COOK TIME: 00 min.

CARBS – 3 g FAT – 0 g PROTEIN – 0 g CALORIES – 141

Ingredients

- 3 cups ice
- 2 ounces tequila
- 1 ounce lime juice
- 2 ½ tsp low-calorie sweetener
- 1 Tbsp coarse salt
- 2 wedge (blank)s lime wedges
- 1 pint-sized Mason jar
- 2 fluid ounces orange-flavored sparkling water

Directions

1. Fill a shaker half-full with ice. Add the lime juice, tequila, and sweetener. Shake for 10-15 seconds until the outside has frosted.
2. Put the salt on a plate. Run a lime wedge along the glass rim. Press the glass down into the salt. Fill it with ice.
3. Strain into the glass. Top with sparkling water and stir. Serve with a lime wedge.

STRAWBERRY BASIL ITALIAN LEMONADE

SERVINGS: 8   PREP TIME: 5 min.   COOK TIME: 00 min.

CARBS – 2 g   FAT – 0 g   PROTEIN – 0 g   CALORIES – 7

Ingredients

- *2 cups strawberries, crushed*
- *2 lemon juice*
- *2 cups ice cubes*
- *2 liters mineral water*
- *2 cups basil leaves, stems removed and divided*

Directions

1. Add the strawberries to a large bowl and crush with a potato masher.
2. Add the lemon juice, stir and set aside.
3. Add the basil leaves to the mineral water and let them soak for 6-8 hours.
4. Add 2 spoonfuls of crushed strawberry to the bottom of the serving glasses. Add the fresh basil leaves and ice cubes. Pour water over the top and serve.

CHOCOLATE MINT AVOCADO SMOOTHIE

SERVINGS: 1   PREP TIME: 5 min.   COOK TIME: 00 min.

CARBS – 10 g   FAT – 44 g   PROTEIN – 26 g   CALORIES – 552

Ingredients

- ½ cup coconut milk
- 1 cup water
- ½ cup ice
- 2 scoops Chocolate Collagen Protein
- ½ frozen avocado
- 4 mint leaves
- 1 Tbsp crushed cacao butter
- 2 Tbsp shredded coconut

Directions

1. Add all of the ingredients (except the protein and shredded coconut) to a blender.
2. Blend for 45 seconds – 1 minute on high speed.
3. Add the protein and blend for 5 more seconds on low.
4. Top with mint leaves and serve.

STRAWBERRY LIMEADE

SERVINGS: 8 PREP TIME: 5 min. COOK TIME: 00 min.

CARBS – 10 g FAT – 16 g PROTEIN – 35 g CALORIES – 16

Ingredients

- *1½ cups strawberries, sliced*
- *¾ cup fresh lime juice*
- *Stevia, to taste*
- *5 cups water*
- *1 cup ice, or more*

Directions

1. Add the strawberries and lime juice to a blender and blend until smooth.
2. Pour the mixture into a pitcher.
3. Add the stevia and water. Mix well.
4. Add ice and serve when cold.

AVOCADO TOMATO SALAD

SERVINGS: 1 PREP TIME: 10 min. COOK TIME: 00 min.

CARBS – 9 g FAT – 10 g PROTEIN – 1 g CALORIES – 105

Ingredients

- *2 cups lettuce*
- *2 tomatoes, sliced*
- *1 avocado, sliced*
- *Shaved Emmental cheese, for garnish*
- *1-2 Tbsp Caesar salad dressing (p. 70)*

Directions

1. Toss the vegetables with the lettuce in a large bowl. Shave cheese over the salad.
2. Add the Caesar dressing and toss well to combine.

CREAMY CUCUMBER SALAD

SERVINGS: 2 PREP TIME: 5 min. COOK TIME: 00 min.

CARBS – 1 g FAT – 12 g PROTEIN – 1 g CALORIES – 116

Ingredients

- *1 cucumber, sliced*
- *2 Tbsp mayo*
- *2 Tbsp lemon juice*
- *Black pepper and salt, to taste*

Directions

1. Mix the cucumber slices, mayo, and lemon juice in a small bowl.
2. Adjust the salt and pepper to taste. Serve.

SMOKED SALMON AND AVOCADO CAESAR SALAD

SERVINGS: 2   PREP TIME: 10 min.   COOK TIME: 00 min.

CARBS – 16 g   FAT – 25 g   PROTEIN – 26 g   CALORIES – 497

Ingredients

- ¼ cup Caesar dressing, or more to taste (p. 72)
- 6 ounces smoked salmon, flaked
- 1 avocado, chopped
- 2 handfuls baby kale leaves or chopped kale stem removed
- 2 handfuls chopped romaine lettuce hearts

Directions

1. Toss all of the salad components in a bowl and pour the Caesar dressing on top.
2. Mix well to coat everything evenly and serve.

LUNCH SALAD WITH TUNA

SERVINGS: 1 PREP TIME: 10 min. COOK TIME: 00 min.

CARBS – 4 g FAT – 32 g PROTEIN – 39 g CALORIES – 464

Ingredients

- 1 can tuna in brine
- 2 Tbsp olive oil
- 2 cup spinach
- 2 Tbsp feta cheese chunks
- 1 ½ tsp Dijon mustard
- ¼ lemon zest

Directions

1. Mix all of the wet ingredients in a small bowl.
2. In another bowl, combine the tuna and spinach.
3. Pour the wet ingredients over the tuna and spinach and mix when ready to eat.

SALMON, AVOCADO AND ARUGULA SALAD

SERVINGS: 2 PREP TIME: 10 min. COOK TIME: 00 min.

CARBS – 11 g FAT – 49 g PROTEIN – 25 g CALORIES – 575

Ingredients

- *3 oz arugula*
- *¼ cup scallions (white part), chopped*
- *8 oz smoked salmon fillet, cooked*
- *1 avocado, diced*
- *1-2 Tbsp lemon dressing*

Directions

1. Add the arugula, salmon, and avocado to a serving bowl.
2. Toss together, then drizzle the lemon dressing over the top.
3. Mix again before serving.

KETO TUNA SALAD WITH AVOCADO

SERVINGS: 2 PREP TIME: 5 min. COOK TIME: 00 min.

CARBS – 7 g FAT – 13 g PROTEIN – 34 g CALORIES – 297

Ingredients

- *¼ cup fresh basil*
- *1 ripe avocado*
- *1 clove garlic*
- *⅛ tsp sea salt*
- *1 tsp lemon juice*
- *1 tsp extra virgin olive oil*
- *1 medium stalk celery, chopped*
- *⅛ red onion medium, chopped*
- *2 cans packed in water tuna, drained*
- *Ground black pepper, to taste*

Directions

1. Blend the basil, sea salt, avocado, garlic, lemon juice, and oil in a food processor until smooth.
2. Add the celery, tuna, and red onion. Pulse minimally, 2 to 3 times, to mix the ingredients.
3. Serve by spreading the tuna salad on lettuce leaves.

STRAWBERRY SPINACH SALAD

SERVINGS: 4 PREP TIME: 15 min. COOK TIME: 00 min.

CARBS – 8 g FAT – 26 g PROTEIN – 3 g CALORIES – 267

Ingredients

- 1½ cup baby spinach
- 1½ cup strawberries, sliced
- 3 Tbsp basil leaves
- ¼ cup pecans or walnuts, toasted and sliced
- ¼ cup feta or goat cheese optional
- 1-2 Tbsp balsamic dressing (p. 63)

Directions

1. Toss the spinach, strawberries, pecans, and cheese in a salad bowl. Top with 2 Tbsp of dressing before serving.

MICROWAVABLE CHEESE CRISPS

SERVINGS: 1 PREP TIME: 5 min. COOK TIME: 00 min.

CARBS – 14 g FAT – 11 g PROTEIN – 28 g CALORIES – 266

Ingredients

- *3 cracker-cut cheese slices*

Directions

1. Put the cheese slices between 2 pieces of parchment paper and transfer onto a microwavable plate.
2. Microwave on high for 2 minutes. Don't take them out. Let them stand for 1 minute.
3. Remove the parchment paper, and transfer the cheese to paper towels to drain.

KETO AVOCADO TOAST

SERVINGS: 4   PREP TIME: 5 min.   COOK TIME: 00 min.

CARBS – 14 g   FAT – 22 g   PROTEIN – 10 g   CALORIES – 438

Ingredients

- *1 large ripe avocado, cut in half*
- *4 chaffles or slices toasted keto bread*
- *½ tsp everything bagel seasoning*
- *Sea salt, to taste*
- *Black pepper, to taste*

Directions

1. Spoon out the flesh of the avocado in a bowl. Mash with a fork until smooth and creamy. Season with salt and pepper.
2. Spread the avocado on top of the toast.
3. Top with bagel seasoning, pepper, and sea salt.

SMOKED SALMON PLATE

SERVINGS: 1 PREP TIME: 10 min. COOK TIME: 00 min.

CARBS – 6 g FAT – 21 g PROTEIN – 31 g CALORIES – 150

Ingredients

- 6 oz. smoked salmon
- ½ cup mayonnaise
- 1 oz. baby spinach
- ½ Tbsp olive oil
- ¼ lime wedges
- Salt and pepper

Directions

1. Put the spinach, salmon, lime, and mayonnaise on a plate.
2. Drizzle the oil over the spinach and season with salt and pepper.

DAIRY-FREE LEMON FAT BOMBS

SERVINGS: 10 PREP TIME: 1 h. COOK TIME: 00 min.

CARBS – 3 g FAT – 16 g PROTEIN – 1 g CALORIES – 164

Ingredients

- ¾ cup coconut butter
- ¼ cup coconut oil
- 3 Tbsp lemon juice
- 1 lemon zest
- 1 Tbsp coconut cream (the thick part of coconut milk)
- 1 tsp vanilla extract
- 1 pinch of salt

Directions

1. Add all of the components to a blender and blend until well-combined.
2. Line a plate with parchment paper. Scoop the bomb mixture out onto the parchment. Freeze for 30 minutes or more until it's firm enough, and you can handle it without melting.
3. Remove from the freezer, roll into balls, and chill in the freezer until set. Enjoy!

AVOCADO TOAST WITH PROSCIUTTO

SERVINGS: 2 PREP TIME: 5 min. COOK TIME: 00 min.

CARBS – 10 g FAT – 15 g PROTEIN – 17 g CALORIES – 330

Ingredients

- 2 slices toasted keto bread or chaffles
- 4 oz prosciutto, divided
- 1 avocado, smashed
- ½ cup arugula
- 1 tsp chives, diced

Directions

1. Spread the avocado on the toasted pieces of bread. Press it a little to mush.
2. Top with the arugula, prosciutto, and chives.

AVOCADO TURKEY TOASTS

SERVINGS: 2 PREP TIME: 10 min. COOK TIME: 00 min.

CARBS – 7 g FAT – 60 g PROTEIN – 22 g CALORIES – 660

Ingredients

- *4-5 slices toasted keto bread*
- *6 oz. deli turkey*
- *1 avocado, sliced*
- *3 oz. non-dairy cream cheese*
- *Salt and pepper*

Directions

1. Spread the cheese on top of the bread slices. Then, mash the avocado and spread it over the cheese. Season with salt and pepper.
2. Top with slices of deli turkey and enjoy.

SALMON AVOCADO TOAST

SERVINGS: 4 PREP TIME: 5 min. COOK TIME: 00 min.

CARBS – 10 g FAT – 11 g PROTEIN – 14 g CALORIES – 432

Ingredients

- 4 slices toasted keto bread
- 1 avocado, sliced
- 8 oz smoked salmon
- 2 Tbsp capers
- 4 Tbsp sour cream
- 1 Tbsp diced chives
- 1 tsp sea salt
- 1 tsp fresh cracked pepper

Directions

1. Layer the avocado onto each slice of bread. Top each slice of bread with salmon.
2. Top with 1 Tbsp chives, sour cream, and capers. Season with salt and pepper.

MICROWAVE PIZZA BREAD

SERVINGS: 1 PREP TIME: 10 min. COOK TIME: 00 min.

CARBS – 7 g FAT – 25 g PROTEIN – 16 g CALORIES – 332

Ingredients

- 1 Tbsp coconut flour
- 1 Tbsp unsalted butter melted
- 1 egg
- 1 Tbsp superfine almond flour
- ⅛ tsp Italian seasoning
- ⅛ tsp baking powder
- 1 Tbsp milk
- 2 Tbsp shredded mozzarella cheese
- 1 Tbsp shredded parmesan cheese
- 1 Tbsp low sugar tomato sauce
- 6-8 mini pepperoni

Directions

1. Add the butter, egg, milk, flours, and baking powder to a large and wide microwave-safe mug. Whisk until it is smooth. Add the seasoning and Parmesan cheese.
2. Cook in the microwave for 90 seconds at full power or more until the bread is cooked.
3. Spread the tomato sauce on top of the bread. Sprinkle with mozzarella cheese. Place pepperoni on top of the cheese.
4. Cook for 30 seconds to melt the cheese.

CHOCOLATE MUG CAKE

SERVINGS: 1 PREP TIME: 5 min. COOK TIME: 00 min.

CARBS – 7 g FAT – 23 g PROTEIN – 9 g CALORIES – 272

Ingredients

- 2 Tbsp almond flour
- 1 Tbsp cocoa powder, sifted
- 1 Tbsp low carb sugar
- ¼ tsp baking powder
- 1 Tbsp cream cheese
- 1 large egg yolk
- 1 tsp water

Directions

1. Measure all of the dry ingredients into a mug and mix well using a fork.
2. Add the cream cheese, egg yolk, and water, stirring to get it all from the bottom. Let it sit for 1-2 minutes.
3. Microwave for 50 seconds or more, depending on your microwave.

NO-BAKE CHOCOLATE PEPPERMINT COOKIE BARS

SERVINGS: 10   PREP TIME: 1 h.   COOK TIME: 00 min.

CARBS – 5 g   FAT – 11 g   PROTEIN – 5 g   CALORIES – 123

Ingredients

FOR THE COOKIE BARS:
- 3 cups shredded coconut
- 2 Tbsp monk fruit
- 2 Tbsp grass-fed ghee
- 6 Tbsp collagen protein
- 4-6 drops food grade peppermint essential oil
- 2 tsp organic chlorella powder
- 3 tsp vanilla extract
- 1 pinch of salt

FOR THE CHOCOLATE DRIZZLE:
- 2 Tbsp cacao powder
- 3 Tbsp ghee or coconut oil, melted
- 1 tsp vanilla extract
- 15 drops liquid stevia

Directions

1. Add the coconut to a blender and blend on a high speed until finely chopped.
2. Add the rest of the cookie bar components (except the collagen), and blend until well combined.
3. Add the collagen and mix on a low speed until incorporated.
4. Line a loaf pan with parchment, scoop out the ingredients into the tin.
5. Press it down evenly with a spoon, then freeze until firm enough to slice.
6. Combine the ingredients for the chocolate drizzle in a small bowl until incorporated.
7. Remove the bars from pan and slice. Drizzle with the chocolate mixture and freeze for 5 more minutes.

CINNAMON ROLL MUG CAKE

SERVINGS: 2 PREP TIME: 5 min. COOK TIME: 00 min.

CARBS – 9 g FAT – 37 g PROTEIN – 12 g CALORIES – 403

Ingredients

- *2 Tbsp avocado oil*
- *3 Tbsp almond meal*
- *1 egg*
- *½ tsp vanilla*
- *½ tsp ground cinnamon*
- *½ tsp baking powder*
- *1 tsp monk fruit*
- *2 Tbsp whipped cream cheese*
- *1 Tbsp water*

Directions

1. Add the oil, almond meal, egg, cinnamon, baking powder, vanilla, and monk fruit in a mug. Mix well with a fork.
2. Put in a microwave and cook for 90 seconds on high.
3. Run a knife around the mug edges and place on a plate.
4. Reuse the same mug, add the cream cheese and water. Microwave for 25 more seconds.
5. Take it out and pour over the cake. Sprinkle with cinnamon.

NO-BAKE GINGER SHORTBREAD COOKIES

SERVINGS: 4 PREP TIME: 20 min. COOK TIME: 00 min.

CARBS – 6 g FAT – 12 g PROTEIN – 6 g CALORIES –157

Ingredients

- *2 vanilla shortbread collagen protein bars*
- *1 Tbsp brain octane oil*
- *1 Tbsp coconut butter, melted*
- *1 tsp ground ginger*
- *¼ tsp grated ginger to garnish*

Directions

1. Add the bars, brain octane, and ginger to a food processor. Blend until it is doughy and not crumbly.
2. Take a full spoon of dough and form a round cookie by pressing it in between your palms. Repeat with the remaining dough.
3. Drizzle the coconut butter over the cookies.

CHOCOLATE KETO ICE CREAM

SERVINGS: 1 PREP TIME: 2-3 h. COOK TIME: 00 min.

CARBS – 10 g FAT – 16 g PROTEIN – 3 g CALORIES – 170

Ingredients

- *13.5 ounce can full-fat coconut milk*
- *1 scoop Chocolate Coconut Collagen Fuel*
- *¼ cup macadamia butter*
- *2 tsp pure vanilla extract*
- *3 Tbsp unsweetened cocoa powder*

Directions

1. Whisk the macadamia butter, coconut milk, collagen fuel, cocoa powder, vanilla, and salt until smooth to make ice cream.
2. Transfer the mixture into the ice cream maker bowl and churn until the desired thickness is reached. Or freeze in the fridge until firm.

EGGNOG CUSTARD

SERVINGS: 8   PREP TIME: 15 min.   COOK TIME: 00 min.

CARBS – 2 g   FAT – 4 g   PROTEIN – 11 g   CALORIES – 122

Ingredients

- *4 eggs*
- *1 cup half and half*
- *½ cup heavy whipping cream*
- *¼ cup Truvia*
- *¼ tsp ground nutmeg*

Directions

1. Blend the eggs, whipping cream, half and half, Truvia, and nutmeg in a blender on low speed. Do not to whip air into the mixture.
2. Transfer the mixture into a 6-cup glass microwave-safe bowl.
3. Cook for 4 minutes at 50% power in the microwave. Stir thoroughly.
4. Cook at 50% power for 3-4 minutes more. Stir well and serve.

MICROWAVE CHEESECAKE

SERVINGS: 1 PREP TIME: 15 min. COOK TIME: 00 min.

CARBS – 4 g FAT – 16 g PROTEIN – 12 g CALORIES – 204

Ingredients

- *2 oz cream cheese, cubed*
- *¼ tsp pure vanilla extract*
- *½ tsp stevia glycerite*
- *1 large egg*

Directions

1. Add the cream cheese to a 3-inch wide ceramic ramekin. Microwave for 15 seconds to soften. Add the vanilla and stevia, mix to combine with a fork.
2. Mix in the egg until smooth. Microwave for 90 seconds.
3. Let it rest and cool in the ramekin, then run a knife around the edges and invert it onto a plate.
4. Top with toppings of your choice and serve.

BALSAMIC DRESSING

SERVINGS: 1   PREP TIME: 10 min.   COOK TIME: 00 min.

CARBS – 2 g   FAT – 2 g   PROTEIN – 3 g   CALORIES – 32

Ingredients

- ½ cup olive oil
- ¼ cup balsamic vinegar
- ¼ cup lemon juice
- ½ tsp thyme
- Salt and pepper to taste

Directions

1. Add all of the components to a jar and shake well.

LEMON-AVOCADO SAUCE

SERVINGS: 2 PREP TIME: 10 min. COOK TIME: 15 min.

CARBS – 47 g FAT – 17 g PROTEIN – 20 g CALORIES – 414

Ingredients

- 1 medium-sized ripe avocado
- 1 tsp lemon zest
- 2 tsp coconut aminos
- 3 Tbsp lemon juice
- 2 Tbsp extra virgin olive oil
- 2 Tbsp chopped fresh parsley
- 1 Tbsp cider vinegar
- Water, depend on thickness
- Sea salt and black pepper, to taste

Directions

1. Mix the lemon zest and juice, parsley, avocado, aminos, olive oil, and vinegar in a food processor.
2. Blend until smooth. Blend in water – 1 Tbsp at a time – until you reach the desired consistency.
3. Season with salt and pepper.

LEMON DRESSING

SERVINGS: 1   PREP TIME: 10 min.   COOK TIME: 00 min.

CARBS – 2 g   FAT – 11 g   PROTEIN – 2 g   CALORIES – 110

Ingredients

- ¼ cup extra virgin olive oil
- 2 tbs lemon juice
- 1 tsp white wine vinegar
- ½ tsp Dijon mustard
- black pepper

Directions

1. To make the dressing, combine all of the components in a bowl or jar.
2. Whisk it vigorously until it is well-combined.

POMEGRANATE VINAIGRETTE DRESSING

SERVINGS: 1 PREP TIME: 5 min. COOK TIME: 00 min.

CARBS – 6 g FAT – 4 g PROTEIN – 0 g CALORIES – 60

Ingredients

- *3 Tbsp Olive oil*
- *1 Tbsp pomegranate juice*
- *½ Tbsp Balsamic vinegar*
- *¼ tsp Garlic salt*
- *Black pepper to taste*

Directions

1. Put all of the ingredients into a jar.
2. Shake until emulsified and ready to use.

SEASON ANYTHING SPICE MIX

SERVINGS: 1 PREP TIME: 5 minutes. COOK TIME: 00 min.

CARBS – 2 g FAT – 1 g PROTEIN – 0 g CALORIES – 8

Ingredients

- *1 cup paprika*
- *⅓ cup onion granules (or onion powder)*
- *⅓ cup chili powder*
- *⅓ cup garlic granules (or garlic powder)*
- *3 Tbsp black pepper*
- *2 Tbsp oregano*
- *2 Tbsp turmeric powder*
- *1 cup salt*

Directions

1. Combine everything in a mason jar.
2. Cover and shake until combined.

EVERYTHING BAGEL SEASONING

SERVINGS: 1 PREP TIME: 5 min. COOK TIME: 00 min.

CARBS – 0 g FAT – 0 g PROTEIN – 0 g CALORIES – 6

Ingredients

- *3 Tbsp sesame seeds*
- *2 Tbsp poppy seeds*
- *1 Tbsp dried minced onion*
- *1 Tbsp dried minced garlic*
- *1 tsp coarse sea salt*

Directions

1. Add everything to a small jar and stir well.
2. Store tightly covered

SEASONED SALT

SERVINGS: 1   PREP TIME: 5 min.   COOK TIME: 00 min.

CARBS – 0 g   FAT – 0 g   PROTEIN – 0 g   CALORIES – 3

Ingredients

- ¼ cup fine sea salt
- 1½ Tbsp ground black pepper
- 1 Tbsp paprika
- 1 tsp garlic powder
- 1 tsp onion powder
- 1 tsp celery salt

Directions

1. Mix all of the components together and keep in a shaker bottle or mason jar.

CAESAR SALAD DRESSING

SERVINGS: 1 PREP TIME: 5 min. COOK TIME: 00 min.

CARBS – 1 g FAT – 7 g PROTEIN – 2 g CALORIES – 17

Ingredients

- 1¼ cups mayonnaise
- 6 Tbsp olive oil
- 2 Tbsp lemon juice
- 2 Tbsp anchovy paste
- 2 Tbsp Worcestershire sauce
- 6 cloves garlic, minced
- Sea salt to taste
- Black pepper to taste

Directions

1. Whisk all of the dressing ingredients together until smooth. Adjust the salt and pepper to taste.

RECIPE INDEX

CONCLUSION

Thank you for reading this book and having the patience to try the recipes.

I do hope that you have had as much enjoyment reading and experimenting with the meals as I have had writing the book.

Stay safe and healthy!

CONVERSION TABLES

Dry Weights

oz	(spoon)	C	(scale) g	(scale) lb
1/2 oz	1 Tbsp	1/16 C	15 g	
1 oz	2 Tbsp	1/8 C	28 g	
2 oz	4 Tbsp	1/4 C	57 g	
3 oz	6 Tbsp	1/3 C	85 g	
4 oz	8 Tbsp	1/2 C	115 g	1/4 lb
8 oz	16 Tbsp	1 C	227 g	1/2 lb
12 oz	24 Tbsp	1 1/2 C	340 g	3/4 lb
16 oz	32 Tbsp	2 C	455 g	1 lb

Liquid Conversions

1 Gallon:
4 quarts
8 pints
16 cups
128 fl oz
3.8 liters

1 Quart:
2 pints
4 cups
32 fl oz
0.95 liters

1 Pint:
2 cups
16 fl oz
480 ml

1 Cup:
16 Tbsp
8 fl oz
240 ml

oz	(spoon) tsp	(spoon) Tbsp	mL	C	Pt	Qt
1 oz	6 tsp	2 Tbsp	30 ml	1/8 C		
2 oz	12 tsp	4 Tbsp	60 ml	1/4 C		
2 2/3 oz	16 tsp	5 Tbsp	80 ml	1/3 C		
4 oz	24 tsp	8 Tbsp	120 ml	1/2 C		
5 1/3 oz	32 tsp	11 Tbsp	160 ml	2/3 C		
6 oz	36 tsp	12 Tbsp	177 ml	3/4 C		
8 oz	48 tsp	16 Tbsp	237 ml	1 C	1/2 pt	1/4 qt
16 oz	96 tsp	32 Tbsp	480 ml	2 C	1 pt	1/2 qt
32 oz	192 tsp	64 Tbsp	950 ml	4 C	2 pt	1 qt

Fahrenheit to Celcius (F to C)

500 F = 260 C
475 F = 245 C
450 F = 235 C
425 F = 220 C
400 F = 205 C
375 F = 190 C
350 F = 180 C
325 F = 160 C
300 F = 150 C
275 F = 135 C
250 F = 120 C
225 F = 107 C

Safe Cooking Meat Temperatures

1 Tbsp: 15 ml
1 tsp: 5 ml

Minimum temperatures:

USDA Safe at 145 F — Beef Steaks, Briskets, and Roasts; Pork Chops, Roasts, Ribs, Shoulders, and Butts; Lamb Chops, Legs, and Roasts; Fresh Hams, Veal Steaks, Fish, and Shrimp

USDA Safe at 160 F — Ground Meats (except poultry)

USDA Safe at 165 F — Chicken & Turkey, ground or whole

CPSIA information can be obtained
at www.ICGtesting.com
Printed in the USA
BVHW051503060221
599512BV00014B/2677